FAMOUS
EXPERIMENTS
AND HOW TO
REPEAT THEM

Also by Brent Filson
EXPLORING WITH LASERS

FAMOUS EXPERIMENTS AND HOW TO REPEAT THEM

Brent Filson

Illustrations by
Brigita Fuhrmann

JULIAN MESSNER   NEW YORK

Published by Julian Messner,
A Division of Simon & Schuster, Inc.
Simon & Schuster Building
Rockefeller Center
1230 Avenue of the Americas
New York, New York 10020

JULIAN MESSNER and colophon are
trademarks of Simon & Schuster, Inc.

Manufactured in the United States of America

Design by Sofia Grunfeld

10 9 8 7 6 5 4

Library of Congress Cataloging-in-Publication Data

Filson, Brent.
    Famous experiments and how to repeat them.

    Bibliography: p
    Includes index.
    Summary: Examines the experiments of Archimedes,
Galileo, Newton, Fleming, and others, whose scientific
efforts gave new ideas to mankind. Includes instructions
for the reader to perform the same experiments.
    1. Science—Experiments—History—Juvenile literature.
    2. Science—Experiments—Juvenile literature.
[1. Science—Experiments—History. 2 Science—Experiments. 3. Experiments] I. Fuhrmann, Brigita, ill.
II. Title.
Q164.F54   1986   507'.8   85-22259
ISBN: 0-671-55687-8

for Michelle Filson

CONTENTS

CHAPTER 1

THE EXPERIMENT: INSTRUMENT OF CHANGE

Let's begin this book about famous experiments by imagining several scenes.

The first is of a Roman general. We see him riding into a defeated city, surrounded by thousands of his soldiers, their helmets and spears flashing in the late afternoon sun. The year is 212 B.C., and the general's army has just conquered Syracuse, one of the most important ports on the Mediterranean. This means that Rome is now the most powerful city in the world.

Let's switch to another scene. On that same day, there is another man in that very same city. He isn't a soldier. He isn't a great leader. He isn't being acclaimed by anyone. Instead, he is old and poor. And while the general leads his troops triumphantly through the city's gates, this man is sitting in his house alone, quietly drawing figures in sand.

Now let's move forward in history and imagine two more scenes. It is 1666, and a plague is ravaging the city of London. The streets are filled with the dead and dying. Many people are convinced that the end of the world has come.

Meanwhile, about 100 miles away in the peaceful English countryside, there is an altogether different scene. In a tiny room of a quaint manor, a young man pulls down a window shade. A thin shaft of sunlight cuts through a hole he made in the shade. The young man holds a piece of glass up to the light. On the wall opposite the glass, many colors suddenly appear. The young man begins to carefully observe the colors.

These contrasting scenes provide an important lesson: human change has come about as much by solitary individuals working without fanfare as by great wars and natural disasters. Today, few people can name the Roman general who rode into Syracuse in 212 B.C. He and his army have all but been forgotten. And the terrible London plague is only a footnote in history. Yet the old man in Syracuse and the young man in England nearly 2000 years later are famous. For the work they both did in quiet solitude has a direct impact on our lives today.

The first man was Archimedes; the second, Isaac Newton. Both of them forged change not by moving armies or conquering cities, but by creating new ideas.

We will take a look at how people like Archimedes and Newton helped create new ideas by conducting scientific experiments.

The scientific experiment is one of the great achievements of Western civilization. Without the experiment, science as we know it could not exist.

Science is obtaining and using knowledge of our physical world. We obtain that knowledge by a special method, called the scientific method. In a sense, the method is a way of thinking. First, a question is asked. Then facts relating to the question are gathered. From the facts a tentative answer is formed. Then that answer is tested, the key part of the method.

An answer cannot become scientific fact until it is tested, until it is proved to be true. The best means to test an answer is by experiment.

An experiment is a way of proving by simply doing. It is a way of turning an idea into physical action.

For instance, in 1654, Otto Von Guericke had an idea that air pressure was very powerful. No one believed him until he proved it by creating a device that was so strongly held together by air pressure that even teams of horses could not pull it apart.

In 1689, Galileo had an idea that objects of different weight fall at the same speeds. He proved it by dropping two objects of different weights from a high place.

In 1831, Michael Faraday thought that electricity could flow from magnetism. But just because he thought it was true did not make it true. It was only when he did an experiment with coiled wire, a magnet, and a voltage recorder that he could prove it.

In most cases, doing the right experiment is not as simple as these illustrations make it seem. Most new experiments fail and must be done over and over. In some instances, a different result than that expected is produced, as you shall see in Chapter 10 about Alexander Fleming.

Whatever the results of the experiment, one factor remains important: The results must be able to be achieved again and again. An experiment is not valid unless it can be repeated.

3

In this book, we will not only examine some of the great experiments of scientific history, but we will show you how to repeat those very same experiments for yourself.

In repeating these famous experiments, you won't be doing anything as dramatic as leading an army or witnessing a great natural catastrophe. But you will be participating in the very actions that have transformed the course of human thought.

A word of caution. The experiments in this book are safe. But in performing any scientific experiment, care must be taken to follow the instructions exactly. This will not only insure that the experiment is done correctly, but that it is done safely too.

One experiment in the book has been omitted. It concerns the experiment Madame Curie did in discovering radium. Repeating Madame Curie's work with pitchblende would be impossible for you to do, as you will see when you read the chapter. Furthermore, radioactive materials can be too dangerous to work with in carrying out an experiment at the beginner's level.

Let's start with an experiment that was conducted about 3000 years ago by people who did not know—or care—that they were experimenting.

CHAPTER 2

THE PYRAMIDS

The Egyptian pyramids, mountains of carefully cut and exactly laid stones, rear out of the desert south of Cairo. They were designed and built as tombs for the pharaohs. But it is not the pharaohs' mummies and the gold and silver riches, once buried in the inner chambers, that have amazed people for thousands of years. Those treasures were looted long ago. Instead, it is the magnificent structures themselves.

Those structures are a result of one of the first great experiments in history. It was done thousands of years ago by the ancient Egyptians, even though they were not aware that they were performing an experiment.

In science today, we test ideas about the nature of our world by doing experiments. But as far as we know, the Egyptians did not try to test their ideas about the nature of their world. Their ideas were based on their religion, which was not questioned. But in overcoming the enormous problem of how to move massive stones with surgical precision, they no doubt had to test different methods. In other words, they had to experiment. In a sense, building the Pyramids was the successful carrying out of an experiment on a massive scale. It is an experiment that you yourself can, on a much smaller scale, repeat.

The ancient Greeks were so awed by the Pyramids that they numbered them as one of the Seven Wonders of the World. They are the only Wonder to have survived down to today. The Hanging Gardens of Babylon have long ago decayed and fallen to ruin. The Colossus of Rhodes, a statue of the Greek god Apollo that stood astride the harbor at Rhodes, was destroyed in an ancient earthquake. The statue of Zeus at Olympia disappeared, a victim of wars and natural disasters.

But the Pyramids remain. Certainly, they have changed. For instance, the three great Pyramids of Giza were once covered with smoothly polished white limestone, making them glisten like mountains of snow through the shimmering desert air. They were surrounded by small pyramids and many statues. They were approached by gleaming stone causeways adorned with granite and limestone.

Today, the Pyramids are brown and reddish-brown, for the limestone coverings no longer exist. Throughout the centuries, they have been stripped away by people wanting the limestone to construct other buildings. Most of the smaller, surrounding Pyramids are gone too, and the causeways have fallen to ruin. But the large Pyramids remain, awesome and inspiring.

One reason they invoke such wonder is the question that people have pondered for thousands of years: How did the Egyptians build these enormous structures with practically their bare hands? They had no earth-moving machines or power-cranes. In fact, they did not even have the wheel.

Enormous indeed! The largest, built by the Pharaoh Khufu some 2600 years ago, measures 755 feet at each side of the base. This means that if the pyramid were lifted into the air, nine football games could be played at the same time on the surface that it rests on, with room left over! This pyramid is 481 feet high and is composed of slabs of stone that weigh about two and a half tons apiece. There are 2,300,000 of these stones. They are so accurately cut that a knife blade cannot pass between their joints. They were transported to the pyramid construction site from quarries as far as 600 miles away.

The existence of ancient tools and pictures in ancient art reveal how the rocks were cut and then transported on boats down the Nile. Evidence exists too that it took more than 100,000 laborers about twenty years to build the structure. But little evidence exists concerning one of the most important questions: How were these massive stone blocks placed one on top of the other?

After all, the sides of the Pyramids are very steep. How could these slabs be lifted up a steep slope hundreds of feet into the air?

The answer lies in the "experiment" that the Egyptians performed. The experiment involved the use of an inclined plane.

This is how many experts believe the blocks were put into place.

After the first blocks were laid, ramps of stone rubble, cemented by river mud, were constructed. The blocks were pulled by men up ramps and put into place. When the pyramid was completed, the ramps were taken down. The stone came into view for the first time and was cleaned and polished—and the pyramid was complete!

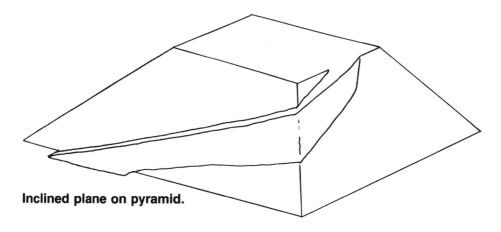

Inclined plane on pyramid.

THE EXPERIMENT:

What you need:

> one rubber band
> a ruler
> four to six large books
> a piece of wood three feet long
> a heavy metal toy car

What you do:

Place the books one on top of the other. Lean the piece of wood against the books. Attach the rubber band to the front of the car. Now turn the car over, so that it rests on its roof. (You do not want to use the car's wheels for this experiment.) Lean the ruler alongside the wood. Now pull the car up the wood, using the rubber band. Measure how far the rubber band stretches when you pull the car up the wood incline.

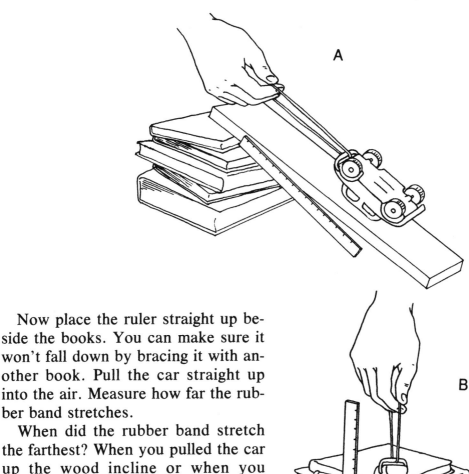

A

B

Now place the ruler straight up beside the books. You can make sure it won't fall down by bracing it with another book. Pull the car straight up into the air. Measure how far the rubber band stretches.

When did the rubber band stretch the farthest? When you pulled the car up the wood incline or when you pulled the car straight up the ruler?

To build their pyramids, the Egyptians used an inclined plane. Bringing an object up a plane requires much less effort than pulling it straight up.

An inclined plane is a kind of machine. A machine is a device that makes work easier. Here is another experiment you can do that uses machines.

Turn the car over so that it rests on its wheels. You can see how much easier it is to pull the car up the inclined plane when it moves on its wheels. You can measure how much easier by using the ruler and the amount of stretch the rubber band makes. Wheels are machines too, because they do work for us.

CHAPTER 3

ARCHIMEDES
(WATER)

The solitary Roman soldier walked through the ruined, smoking streets of ancient Syracuse with sword drawn. He and his fellow soldiers had fought their way into the city only yesterday. As yet, not all the enemy soldiers had been killed or captured. Some were still hiding. The soldier's sword was ready for a surprise attack.

He stopped at a house and pounded the butt of his sword against the wooden door. "Open up," he shouted, "General Marcellus has sent me!"

Marcellus was the Roman leader who led the attack against Syracuse. It had been a long and difficult attack. The Romans had sailed into the harbor to capture the city three years before. They thought the task would be easy. Syracuse's army was weak. It was no match

for the Romans. But the Syracuse people had surprises in store for the Romans. On the day the ships first approached the city, great beams of light suddenly shot toward them. The beams came from huge mirrors planted on top of the tall harbor walls. The mirrors were reflecting the light of the sun. When the light beams struck the ships' sails and wooden hulls, the vessels burst into flames and sank. The undamaged Roman ships fled the harbor.

But the Romans were determined to capture Syracuse. They returned when clouds covered the sun, making the mirrors ineffective. But the Romans were in for more surprises. As they approached the walls again, long poles were pushed out from openings. Some of the poles carried enormous boulders that dropped on the ships, smashing them. Other poles had large hooks that grabbed the ships and overturned them. The Romans thought they were battling titans.

It did not take just a few days to capture Syracuse, as the Romans thought it would. Instead, it had taken three years. Those war machines had allowed a weaker army to hold off a stronger one.

When the Romans finally fought their way into Syracuse, General Marcellus sent a young soldier to bring him the man who had invented the machines. "His name is Archimedes. He is one of the greatest thinkers of all ages," he told the soldier. "I don't want him harmed. I just want to meet this great man."

When he received no answer at the house of this man, the soldier became angry. He burst into the house and found an old man sitting on the floor doing mathematical problems in sand.

"Are you Archimedes?" the soldier demanded.

"Please don't bother me," the old man said. "Can't you see I'm trying to solve a problem?"

"Come with me. General Marcellus wants to meet you."

"I'm too busy to see your general!"

"You don't disobey a Roman!" The soldier growled and drove his sword into the old man.

Archimedes, the greatest thinker and inventor of his time, fell over, dead.

In a way, Archimedes died the way he lived—lost in thought. Throughout his long life, Archimedes put science and mathematics before everything else. (The engines of war that had held off the powerful Romans were, he said, just toys.) Many times he went without sleeping and eating because he was thinking about mathematical problems. It was his ability to think deeply that helped produce one of the great experiments of science.

This happened when Archimedes was a young man. At that time, the king of Syracuse, Hiero II, had just bought a new gold crown. But Hiero had a nagging thought. "I gave my goldsmith a brick of gold and he made a crown out of it. But what if he kept some of the gold for himself? What if he put some silver in with the gold?"

The king summoned Archimedes, who was just becoming renowned as a great scientist. "How can I tell if my goldsmith is honest?" Hiero asked.

Archimedes thought for awhile. He said, "Since gold weighs more than silver, we could compare the weight of your crown to the weight of a crown that we know is pure gold and that is exactly the same size and shape. But, of course, that wouldn't be practical. Or we could melt the crown into a brick and compare it with the same size brick of pure gold. That way we would gain the answer, but lose your crown. It's a difficult problem. But I'll solve it!"

Archimedes left the king and walked the streets of Syracuse, lost in thought. He walked so much that he became hot and tired and decided to take a bath to refresh himself.

As he lowered himself into the tub, his mind still wrestling with the problem, he saw something that made him start. The water rose up and spilled over the edge. "Eureka!" he shouted. "I have it. I have the answer!" He was so excited that he leaped up and ran through the streets shouting, "Eureka! Eureka!" (Eureka means "I've found it!" in Greek.)

Archimedes indeed had found the answer, and here is what it was and how he found it.

Archimedes obtained three containers of water, each the same size and filled to the same level. In the first, he put in pure gold that weighed as much as the crown. In the second, he put in pure silver that weighed as much as the crown. In the third, he placed the crown.

Observing how water spilled over the sides when he lowered his body into the tub, he had realized that an object displaced water. In other words, as his body went *down* into the water, the water pushed *up*. By experimenting with different materials, Archimedes learned that two things cause water to be displaced: weight and volume. The heavier an object is (the more it weighs) and the bigger an object is (the more volume it has), the more water it will displace.

Archimedes knew that gold weighs more than silver. Thus a bigger piece of silver would displace the same amount of water as a smaller piece of gold.

Archimedes found that the crown displaced more water than the same weight in gold. That meant that its volume was greater than the gold volume. The conclusion was obvious: The crown was made of both silver and gold. King Hiero had been cheated.

THE EXPERIMENT:

What you need:

> a string
> a fist-sized stone
> a spring scale
> a bucket of water

What you do:

If you cannot obtain a spring scale from your kitchen at home, you may be able to borrow one from your science room at school.

B

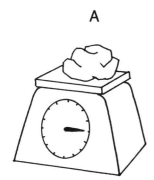

A

Weigh the stone outside the water. Then tie a string around the stone and weigh it in the bucket of water. What is the difference in the weight of the stone out of the water and in the water? Why is there a difference in the weight? What happens to the water when the stone is lowered into it? Remember it was the action of the water in the tub that gave Archimedes his great idea 2300 years ago.

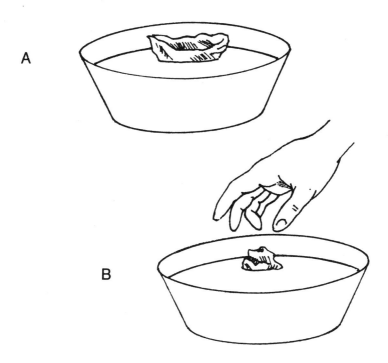

Here is another experiment that can prove that both weight and volume cause water to be displaced. Take a sheet of aluminum foil. Shape it into a boat and float it in water. Now wad the aluminum up. Drop it in the water. By wadding the aluminum up, did you change

17

the weight? Did you change the volume? What happened to the wadded-up foil in the water? Why did it happen?

Here is a final experiment. Place an empty can inside a bucket. Fill the can to the top with water. Make sure no water spills over the side. Weigh the stone outside the water. Now put the stone in the can of water, this time allowing the water to spill over. Remove the can of water. Take the stone out and empty the can. Place the empty can on a kitchen scale. Make a note of the empty can's weight. Then pour the water from the bucket into the can on top of the scale. Make a note of the weight. Subtract the weight of the empty can from the weight of the water-filled can. What is the figure you get? Is it the weight of the stone? Or is it the weight the stone lost when placed in the water?

A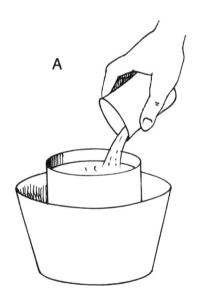

B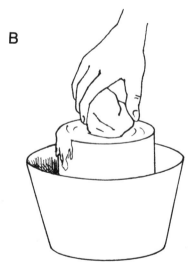

CHAPTER 4

GALILEO
(MOTION)

The 179-foot tall Leaning Tower of Pisa is one of the most famous structures in the world. Without knowing it, the builders constructed the tower on soft ground. During the 800 years of its existence, therefore, the Leaning Tower of Pisa has been ever so slowly toppling over. Today it leans over about seventeen feet from a straight up-and-down line.

But the tower is not just famous for its crazy tilt. It is famous for being the legendary spot where a great scientific experiment was conducted. It was an experiment that smashed an 1800-year-old idea and marked a turning point in scientific investigation. Yet it also helped turn popular opinion against the man who conducted the experiment.

The man was Galileo Galilei, a twenty-five-year-old mathematics professor at the University of Pisa. Though his father had sent him to school to be a doctor, Galileo's main interests were science and mathematics. He was both intensely curious and creative. For instance, eight years before he conducted the famous experiment we will examine, he was kneeling in church at prayer one morning and noticed a chandelier swinging back and forth. That sight filled his mind with questions. The questions prompted him to carry out experiments timing a weight swinging at the end of a string with the beats of his pulse. The experiments led to the discovery of the principle of the pendulum: The distance a pendulum swings may vary, but the time it takes to make the swings is always the same. It was a great discovery, one that led to a new way of making clocks and gave birth to a revolutionary branch of science, dynamics, which deals with motion and force.

That single discovery alone would have made him famous. But Galileo made many other major scientific discoveries. One of those discoveries happened on a day in 1589 when he stood on top of the Leaning Tower of Pisa and dropped two iron balls.

Some historians claim that he did not conduct the experiment on the famous tower. They say he used another high place. We probably will never know for sure. But for our purposes, let us believe that it was the Leaning Tower of Pisa on which he stood that day. For the tower, tilting as it does, provided an ideal laboratory for what Galileo wanted to prove.

This is what he wanted to prove. For nearly 2000 years, people believed that heavy objects fall faster than light objects. They believed, for instance, that if you drop an object weighing ten pounds, it would actually fall ten times faster than an object weighing one pound. Galileo set out to prove that this belief was false.

He trudged up the circular staircase of the tower with baskets filled with iron balls. Some of the balls weighed ten pounds each. Others weighed only one pound. Standing on top of the tower, Galileo held a heavy ball in one hand, a light ball in the other. Then he dropped them.

At the bottom of the tower, a crowd of people craned their necks. The crowd consisted of students and teachers of the University of

21

Pisa. Convinced that the heavy ball would fall to earth much faster than the lighter ball, they were in a scornful mood.

Up until then, people believed that heavy objects fell faster than light objects for one simple reason: A great philosopher had once written that it was so. The philosopher's name was Aristotle. He lived in ancient Greece and was once the tutor of the greatest conqueror of the ancient world, Alexander the Great. Aristotle studied many things: plants, animals, ethics, the theater, astronomy, geography, and politics. He wrote 400 volumes. Some forty volumes of Aristotle's writing exist today. For nearly 2000 years after his death, few people dared to question his views.

But Galileo did. He was considered a crackpot by a lot of people in Pisa. For he argued against many of Aristotle's conclusions. Because of this, he was given the derisive name, "The Wrangler."

As soon as "The Wrangler" Galileo dropped the two balls, laughter broke out among the people at the base of the tower. They knew that he would finally be proved a fool. But the laughter suddenly died. The ten-pound ball and the one-pound ball fell side by side down the length of the tower—and hit the ground at the same time!

The crowd gaped in amazed silence. Galileo had just proved Aristotle wrong!

How could Aristotle have been wrong about the speed of falling objects? The answer is that Aristotle never tested his idea. He developed it because it seemed reasonable. And people believed him. But Galileo did a simple, but tremendously important thing. He did not rely on Aristotle for his conclusions. Instead, he *showed* what happened when a light object and a heavy object were dropped side by side. In other words, he performed an experiment. And he maintained that the results of the experiment, not the conclusions of Aristotle, were what counted. Galileo saw for himself! And in doing so, he made a great advancement in the scientific method.

But few students or professors at the university were won over by the experiment. They considered his reliance on experiments instead of on Aristotle not only wrong, but heresy.

For the rest of his life, even though he performed other important experiments and made findings that were landmarks in physics and astronomy, Galileo was hounded by religious and political leaders. In fact, at the end of his life, the church forced him to renounce his most important and revolutionary idea, that the earth and planets revolve around the sun.

But his discoveries lived after him. Today Galileo is considered one of the great scientists——and experimenters—of the ages.

THE EXPERIMENT:

What you need:

> a baseball
> a rubber ball the size of a baseball, but lighter

What you do:
Station a friend on the ground outside a building. Go up one story to a window and drop the balls at the same time so that they fall near your friend. Make sure your friend stands a safe distance away and looks *and* listens. Make sure your friend sees which ball strikes the ground first. Repeat the experiment several times. Do you get the same results that Galileo did 400 years ago?

Here is an experiment that will show you another important aspect of gravity. All you need are two marbles and a table. Place one marble on the edge of the table. Hold the other marble between your

23

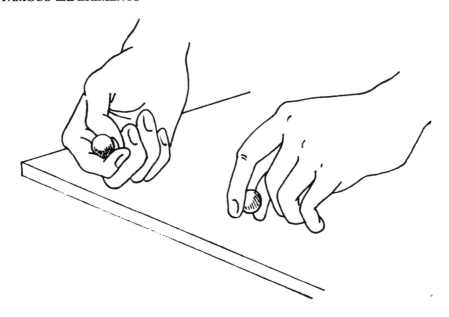

thumb and finger just off the table edge. Now at the same time flick the marble on the table with your finger and drop the other marble. What you have done is caused one marble to fall straight to the floor while you have propelled the other marble straight out into the air. Now listen for which marble lands first. You may think that the marble that dropped straight to the floor would land first because it traveled the least distance. But if you perform the experiment correctly, you will hear both marbles land at the same time.

No matter how far you flick the one marble away from the table, it will take the same time for it to drop to the floor as the other marble. This shows that the force of gravity acts the same on objects whether they are moving forward or falling straight down. In other words, once you flicked the marble off the edge of the table, it became a falling object, just like the object you dropped. Both objects were subject to the same pull of gravity.

As you know, not all objects fall to the ground at the same rate of speed. A sheet of paper falls more slowly than a marble. This is not because gravity pulls differently on different objects (Galileo and your experiments proved that false), but because the paper has a larger surface than the marble. Air pushes up against that surface and slows the paper's fall. Take the same sheet of paper and crumple it up. It will fall faster than when it was not crumpled. But it is air—not gravity—that causes the change in the rate of fall. If the sheet of paper and the marble were put in a vacuum, where there was no air to create resistance, they would both fall at the same rate of speed.

CHAPTER **5**

ISAAC
NEWTON
(LIGHT)

The years were 1665 and 1666, and the Black Death was sweeping across England. The Black Death, a form of bubonic plague caused by the bite of fleas that live on rats, almost always kills its victims. It had struck Europe many times in the past. In the fourteenth century it had killed a quarter of the population. In the summer of 1665, about 31,000 Londoners died of the disease. The dead were piling up so quickly in the streets that not enough able-bodied people could be found to bury them all. What's more, the Black Death was spreading outside of the city. People in the countryside were beginning to panic, thinking that they would be the next victims. Fearful that the plague would strike in their midst, Cambridge

University officials had closed the school and sent its teachers and students home.

One of those teachers was an undistinguished, shy, stocky, twenty-four-year-old country lad. When Cambridge closed, he went to live with his widowed mother on her small manor called Woolsthorpe. "The country air is too healthy for the plague to take root here," his mother told him. "You can carry on your studies without worry until Cambridge reopens."

The teacher lived in a closetlike room in the second story of the manor. During the two years of the English plague, this man, deep in the English countryside, isolated from other scientists, would change the face of mathematics and science for all time.

Here he formulated the idea of gravity.

Here he invented a system of mathematics that we call calculus.

Here he made important discoveries about the nature of light.

And here he laid the groundwork for making the experiment the basis for all scientific advancement.

His name was Isaac Newton. In the decades to come, he would pile achievement upon achievement. When he died at eighty-four, he would be considered, as he is now, one of the greatest scientific minds of all time. But even he admitted that the years 1665 and 1666 were his most creative. "I was in the prime of my age for invention and minded mathematics and philosophy more than any time since," he recalled.

That a solitary young man working outside the academic world would change science more in two years than it had been changed in the previous 2500 years is remarkable. What is equally remarkable is that he used the simplest of methods and devices.

An apple thudding against the ground as he sat under a tree caused him to think: "Why doesn't the moon fall to the ground too?" That question led to his development of the law of gravity and the movements of planets.

With two simple prisms that he bought at a country fair, a reflecting screen, and a window shade, he conducted an experiment that exploded the ages-old conception of the nature of light.

Let's examine that experiment and then show how you can repeat it.

Newton became interested in light through his interest in telescopes. Telescopes had been invented more than a half century before. But they had one persistent flaw. Because the fringe of the lens was always outlined with blurred colors, objects could not be brought into fine focus.

In his tiny room at Woolsthorpe, Newton set about to find out why.

The fringe of a telescope lens acts as a kind of prism. A prism is a clear object whose sides are parallel. Newton decided to examine exactly what happens to light when it passes through a prism.

It was obvious that light entered one side of a prism white and came out the other side multicolored. This had been known for thousands of years. But for thousands of years, people thought light changed from white to rainbow colors because it was darkened differently at the various angles of the prism, that the colors were merely modified forms of white light.

Aided by his experiment, Newton made a simple but revolutionary observation. He noted that light wasn't simply darkened or modified by the prism, but actually *separated* into individual rays of colors. Thus, each color wasn't a form of white light, but a separate thing itself. White light did not exist as people for thousands of years had thought it did, as an absolute phenomenon. Instead, Newton proved, it existed *only as a sum of colors*!

28

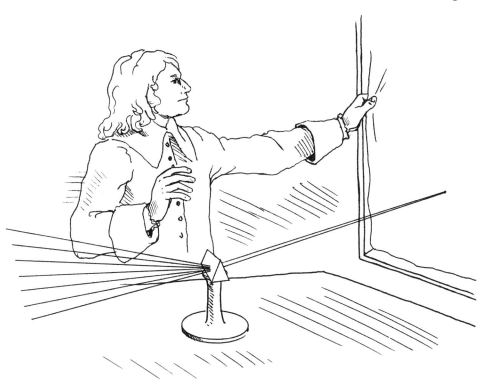

This is how Newton did the experiment. He allowed light to shine into a darkened room through a small, round hole in the window shade. The beam of light was then aimed into a prism. The colors that emerged from the prism were directed to a white screen.

What Newton saw were colors, of course, but something else as well. He saw that the *shape* of the light pattern on the screen was *oblong*. This meant that the light beam that emerged from the prism was oblong too. But remember, it was a round beam that had entered the room through the hole in the shade. It was a round beam

29

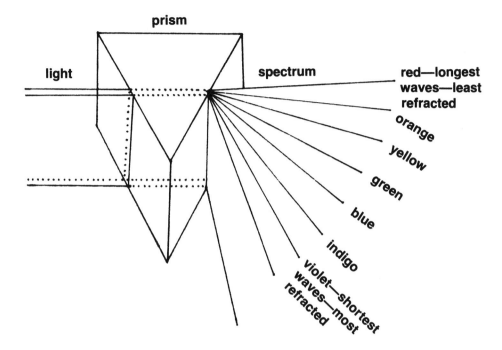

that had entered the prism. How had a round beam changed in the prism to an oblong beam?

Newton correctly concluded that the oblong shape on the screen was caused by the light rays changing direction as they struck the different angles of the prism and fanned out. This change of direction of a light ray is called *refraction*. Each color, he concluded, was defined by the amount of refraction. For instance, red is refracted less than blue.

But Newton did not end the experiment there. In fact, the crucial part of the experiment was what he did next. He placed a second prism in front of the first. The light beam went through the shade into the first prism and then into the second prism. It emerged from the second prism and fell on the screen. The light that fell on the screen was white!

In other words, each color, once separated out by refraction, could not be further separated. Newton had proved that rays of different colors form the basic foundations of light. Each ray of color differs absolutely from the other by how much it can be bent.

THE EXPERIMENT:

What you need:

> a three-sided prism
> a large, black cloth
> a screen (a sheet or blank wall will also work)

What you do:

If you do not have a prism in your home, you may be able to get one from a science kit or from your science room at school.

Use a room with a single window where sunlight enters. Cover the window with the cloth. Put a small, round hole in the cloth, letting a beam of sunlight in. Hold the prism to the beam and direct the beam to the screen. Do you see what Newton did when he conducted this experiment? What shape is the light pattern on the screen? What colors do you see? Why has the white light been changed into a beam of many colors?

You may not be able to obtain a three-sided prism. But you can still perform two experiments that will create a spectrum of colors. The first is to put a glass of water on a windowsill where sunlight is shining in. Look carefully at the light behind the base of the glass. You should see a spectrum of colors. Remember what Newton said

31

about white light being only a combination of the primary colors. What colors do you see?

The second experiment will allow you to see a much clearer spectrum. Put an inch or so of water into a tray and then place the tray on the sunny windowsill. Now rest a mirror on the side of the tray farthest from the windowsill. Observe the light that reflects off the mirror.

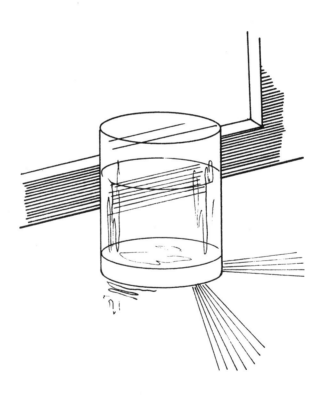

OTTO VON GUERICKE (AIR)

We take for granted what Newton proved more than three centuries ago, that normal light is composed of many colors. Back then, Newton's new ideas practically turned the scientific community on its ear. Some scientists agreed immediately with Newton, but others attacked his conclusions. Newton became annoyed that his critics were arguing from their individual notions of what they thought color was, not from the results of his experiments. Like Galileo before him, he insisted that the facts proven by his experiments were what counted, not individual notions.

Newton was right. The facts could not be refuted. In a few years, the controversy died down, and his ideas were accepted.

Newton's experiments with light were vital steps in the progress of science, not only because they revealed the nature of the color spectrum but because they helped establish rigorous experimentation as the key to scientific questioning. Until his experiments with light, most scientists came to conclusions by mixing their personal notions with the superficial examination of facts. But Newton showed that such notions had no place in science. He showed that facts should not fit the molds of preconceived notions, but that notions should be molded to facts. In other words, scientific truth can only flow from what best tests facts, the experiment.

Newton was angered by the controversy his experiments on light caused. The effort to refute his critics took time from other work he wanted to do. For years afterwards, he kept most of his investigations secret.

By conducting his experiments in private, Newton was following a time-honored tradition of science. For experimentation is usually a solitary endeavor, carried out away from the public arena.

But a few famous experiments have been conducted in public. Galileo's dropping the iron balls from a high place is one example. Another man used public displays of experiments to gain quick acceptance of his ideas.

He was Otto von Guericke, a German burgomaster and engineer who was a genius—both as a scientist and as a showman. He devised a famous experiment that was performed in 1654 before the emperor of the Holy Roman Empire and his court, an experiment that revealed in a startling way the tremendous strength of air pressure.

The ancient Greeks knew that air was a substance that could exert pressure. The Greek philosopher Empetocles asserted that a water clock worked by the pressure air exerted on water. In the first half of the 1600s, Galileo and other scientists made devices that measured the pressure of the air. But until von Guericke performed his experiment, people did not know how really powerful air pressure was.

Von Guericke took two copper hemispheres, greased their rims, and fit them together. With the emperor and nobles watching, he pulled them apart and fit them together several times to show how easily it could be done. Then with a special pump he had invented, he sucked air from the sphere they formed. He attached two horses

on opposite sides of the hemispheres, then gave a signal for the animals to begin pulling. Teamsters cracked whips in the air and shouted. The horses lurched forward, clods of soil flying. The spectators gasped. The hemispheres no longer came apart. They held tightly together. Von Guericke then had four horses on each side try to pull the hemispheres apart. The horses strained and strained, but could not break them apart. It wasn't until sixteen horses, eight pulling from each side, were hitched to the sphere that it finally separated!

35

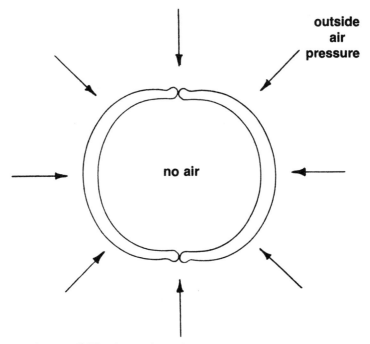

Why was it so difficult to break open the hemispheres? Though people knew that air exerts pressure, they did not know how powerful that pressure was.

The world is wrapped in a sea of air. That sea weighs one million billion tons! Of course, all that weight isn't pressing on you. But the small part that does exerts a weight of fifteen pounds per square inch. That means for every square inch of surface, there is an equivalent of fifteen pounds of air pressing against it. This pressure is called atmospheric pressure.

You might think that with all this weight of air, things would be crushed. But air exerts pressure in all directions. We live in a world where the pressure is always equalized. A bubble is round because

36

the air inside pushes equally against its whole surface. But Von Guericke made a small but significant alteration in the air. He pumped air out of the space inside the sphere. This means that there was no air to press outward. All the air pressure was inward. And the pressure was fifteen pounds per square inch. Tons of air were preventing the sphere from being pulled apart.

THE EXPERIMENT:

What you need:

two rubber plungers

What you do:

Wet the rims of the plungers. Push the plungers together. Now you and a friend try to pull them apart. Make sure that your back is to a wall to prevent you from falling over when the plungers finally do break loose. On a small scale, you have repeated Von Guericke's experiment that amazed the Holy Roman Emperor and his court. What prevented the plungers from coming apart easily?

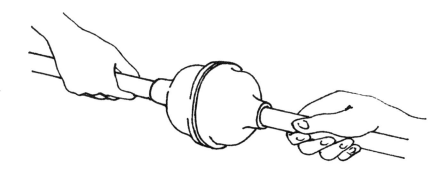

To conduct another experiment with air pressure, you need a tea kettle, a stove, a bottle, and a banana. Fill the kettle with water and put the kettle on the heated stove until the water is boiling. Now direct steam from the boiling water into the bottle. Be careful to use oven gloves so you don't burn your hands. Place the tip of a partially peeled banana into the mouth of the bottle. Observe what happens.

The banana should be sucked into the bottle. Since the steam forced air out of the bottle and created a partial vacuum, what forced the banana into the bottle?

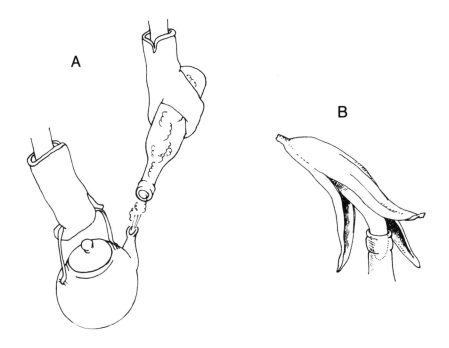

A

B

CHAPTER 7

MICHAEL FARADAY (*ELECTRICITY*)

E very experiment has two vital aspects: its results and the person observing those results. The best experiment is only as good as its observer. There is no better example of this than the experiment Michael Faraday performed in 1831 that changed magnetism into electricity. In regard to how we live today, it may be the most important experiment of all. It might have been a failure if Faraday had been looking elsewhere for only an instant.

It is hard to imagine how we would exist without electricity. Think of all the things we would *not* have without electricity. There would be no radio. No television. No telephones. No movies. No jet aircraft. No flights into space. No kitchen appliances.

Our complex electrical world all flows from Faraday's one experiment.

Michael Faraday was born in 1791 in England, the son of a blacksmith. He grew up in one of the most turbulent times of history, when the Napoleonic Wars were rocking Europe and the Industrial Revolution was taking root in England. But young Faraday was not involved in either of these historic movements, for his youth was spent apprenticing to a bookbinder. Bookbinding did not interest Faraday, but it did provide a window to the exciting happenings of the outside world. For Faraday read many books. He became interested in science, especially electricity.

He read that the ancient Greeks had known about electricity several thousand years before. They would rub amber with cloth and the amber would then attract small particles of lint and straw. The force that made the objects stick to the amber was electricity. (In fact, the word electricity comes from the Greek word "electron" meaning "amber.")

He read about the great experiments with electricity of the previous century and a half. He read about Von Guericke making a globe of sulphur which, when rotated, made crackling noises, glowed, and attracted small objects.

He read about the Leyden jar, a simple device to store and use electricity. In France, a scientist lined up 700 monks hand in hand and had one monk grasp the rod of a Leyden jar. The electricity surged from the jar—and all 700 monks leaped into the air in pain and surprise, each having received a simultaneous shock.

Faraday read about how Benjamin Franklin proved that lightning was electrical. Franklin flew a kite in a rainstorm, and when lightning struck it, he touched a brass key at the end of the kite string. Luckily for Franklin, it was a small burst of lightning. A

40

large burst would have killed him. As it was, Franklin received a strong shock.

Faraday read about Luigi Galvani, the Italian anatomy professor who caused the legs of dead frogs to suddenly twitch when touched with instruments composed of two different metals. Galvani concluded that frogs' legs contain "animal electricity."

Faraday read about another Italian, Allesandro Volta, who built the first electric battery.

Finally, Faraday read about the work of the English scientist Sir Humphry Davy. Davy made the first electric light. He was considered one of the great scientists of the age. But when asked toward the end of his life what his greatest achievement was, he said: "Finding Michael Faraday."

For Faraday did not become a bookbinder. Instead, excited by the books he had read, he applied for a job as a laboratory assistant to Davy at London's Royal Institution. It was a somewhat bold move on Faraday's part, because bookbinding would have provided a secure living. Pay was poor and advancement uncertain for a scientist in those days. But Faraday soon proved a valuable assistant and, in fact, made important discoveries in chemistry himself.

But electricity was his chief interest.

In 1820 Hans Oersted made a discovery that dazzled scientists. He found that when he passed an electrical current through a wire be-

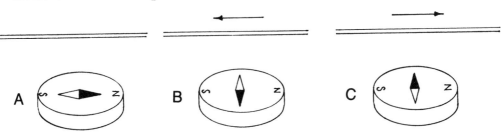

side a compass needle, the needle swung toward it at right angles. When he reversed the current, the needle swung back at right angles. This was the first time that people linked electricity and magnetism.

The exciting thing about Oersted's discovery was that it demonstrated that magnetism could be made from electricity. The discovery led William Sturgeon to invent the electromagnet in 1825. Sturgeon wrapped copper wire around an ordinary iron horseshoe. When he sent an electrical current into the horseshoe, the iron turned into a magnet. This led Michael Faraday to ask a momentous question: If magnetism can be made from electricity, why can't electricity be made from magnetism? He tried four experiments to answer the question. They all failed. But he was determined to go on. He told a friend that he would find the answer even if it took a lifetime of work. It was his fifth experiment that was a success. He found a way of making electricity out of magnetism. It was a great experiment, but it worked only because he happened to glance at the right place at the right time!

Here is Faraday's experiment.

He had an iron ring made, seven-eighths of an inch thick and six inches in diameter. Around one side of the ring he wound a strand of copper wire. He connected the ends of the strand to a battery. Around the other side of the ring he wound another strand of copper wire. He joined the ends to a galvanometer. A galvanometer is a device that detects an electric current. Faraday believed the current from the battery would enter the ring and magnetize it. The iron ring would become an electromagnet. Current then would flow from the electromagnet to the galvanometer. If his experiment worked, the needle of the galvanometer would jump.

Imagine Faraday's excitement as he started to perform his exper-

42

iment. His four earlier experiments had failed, but he had given a great deal of thought to this one. If he succeeded, if the galvanometer's needle jumped, Faraday knew he would have made scientific history.

But when he connected the wire to the battery, a strange thing happened. The needle moved, but only for an instant. It immediately returned to the ''no current'' position. Faraday must have thought he had failed. The connections were made properly, but no current was flowing to the galvanometer. He decided to try again. As he unhooked the wire at the battery, another odd thing happened. The needle moved briefly once more. If Faraday had not kept his eye on the needle, he might have thought his experiment was a complete failure. But he remembered that the needle moved when he first hooked the wire to the battery. This meant that current had flowed briefly to the galvanometer. Somehow that current was connected to his hooking and unhooking the wire to the battery.

Faraday was sure he had produced electricity out of magnetism, but only for brief moments. To see if he could produce a continuous current, he tried other experiments. The results were always the

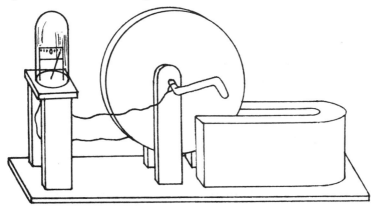

same. The moment he magnetized an iron rod with electricity, the needle would jump, but only for a moment.

For six weeks Faraday kept refining his experiments. Finally, he decided to do away with the iron ring and use only the wire. He coiled it around a copper tube and pushed a magnet inside. The galvanometer moved. When he pulled the magnet out, the needle moved again. When he kept moving the magnet in and out, the needle continued to move. A continuous electrical current was created. Faraday had achieved what he was after.

The key was *motion*. When the magnet and the electrified coil were moving toward each other—or away from each other—electricity was produced. When they were stationary, no electricity was produced. If Faraday had not kept a sharp eye on his original experiment, he might not have discovered this.

Faraday then built a device to provide a continuous electrical current.

Our giant electricity-producing dynamos are based on this device.

THE EXPERIMENT:

What you need:

> bell wire (wire used for telephones; can be obtained at a hardware store)
> a glass
> a compass
> a bar magnet

What you do:
Wrap fifty or sixty turns of wire around a drinking glass. Slip the

wire off the glass and tie the roll of wire with more wire or tape. Wrap the other end of the wire about twenty-five to thirty turns around a compass. Now run the bar magnet in and out of the circle of wire. Watch the compass when you do this. When does the needle move? When is it at rest? What causes the needle to move?

Here are two simple experiments that will create static electricity. (1) Rub a blown-up balloon on your hair or on flannel or fur. If you rub briskly enough, the balloon will stick to a wall or your hand. (2) Place a sheet of paper flat against a wall. Rub the paper with a ruler. After a while, the paper will stick to the wall. Why do the paper and balloon stick to things when they are rubbed? What does this tell you about static electricity?

A final experiment will allow you to actually see the pattern of a magnetic field. You will need a magnet, a piece of cardboard, and iron filings. (Iron filings can be obtained from a chemistry kit or from your science room at school.) Spread the filings on the cardboard and then place the magnet underneath. Observe the filings. What does their pattern tell you about magnetism?

CHAPTER 8

CHRISTIAN JOHANN DOPPLER (SOUND)

A railroad train, trumpeters, and a group of musicians with perfect pitch—these are the ingredients that go into this famous experiment. It's an experiment that has led to dramatic results today. For the principle it proved is used by astronomers examining the universe, in highly sophisticated navigation, and in space craft equipment.

The principle was developed by Christian Johann Doppler. Doppler was an Austrian professor of mathematics who taught in the mid-nineteenth century in a university at Prague. He had a deep interest in colors and sounds.

It was becoming known then that colors as well as sounds were made up of waves. Doppler was interested in those waves. But he was interested in them in a way that few scientists had been before. He wanted to study color and sound waves by how they were *perceived*. In other words, color and sound were important to him only in the way that people experienced them.

In 1842, he wrote one of the most important papers ever produced in the history of science. It was called, "The Changing Light of Double Stars." Double stars are stars that orbit each other. Scientists could not understand why these stars always seemed to be changing colors. In the paper, Doppler said he had the answer. He said that when an object giving off light or sound moves toward us or away from us, the light or sound is changed. The waves strike us more frequently (if the object moves toward us) or less frequently (if it moves away).

Doppler's idea was very simple. His equations to prove the idea were very simple too. In fact, the idea and the equations were so simple that many scientists thought they were foolish. They said they would never be proven.

But a young Dutch meteorologist named Christoph Hendrik Didericus Buys-Ballot proved Doppler's ideas in one of the most unusual experiments of history.

He obtained the use of a locomotive and a flatcar. He put a group of trumpeters on the car. He stationed a number of musicians along the tracks. These musicians possessed perfect pitch. For two days, the flatcar with the trumpeters blowing their horns moved past the musicians at different speeds. The musicians recorded the notes from the trumpets.

The result: Doppler was right. The trumpeting became higher pitched as the locomotive approached the musicians. It became more deeply pitched as it moved away from them. The sound changed

47

depending on the movement and location of the objects giving off the sound.

Doppler said that this effect would also be true with light waves. But some of his calculations were wrong, and it wasn't until 1849 that a French scientist, Armand Fizeau, corrected Doppler's calculations so that they held true for light as well.

Today, the Doppler Effect has vital uses in research and engineering. For instance, it helped astronomers prove that galaxies are flying away from each other, and thus the universe is expanding. And its help in providing more accurate navigation for aircraft and space ships has been invaluable.

THE EXPERIMENT:

What you need:

> a bicycle
> a playing card
> a clothespin
> electrician's tape

What you do:

Turn the bicycle upside down. Place the card in the clothespin and tape the pin to the spoke of the bicycle. As you spin the wheel, the spoke should strike the card, making it flap and make noise. Spin the wheel slowly. Listen to the noise the card makes. Is it high pitched or low pitched? Now spin the wheel faster. Again listen to the noise. How is it different from the noise that the card made when the wheel spun slowly?

Now spin the wheel as fast as you can. Listen to the noise the card makes. Why has there been a change in the noise? To answer that question, remember what Doppler said: When an object emitting sound approaches you, the sound waves pile up and the sound becomes higher pitched. The flapping card, of course, wasn't approaching you, but the theory applies because the more rapidly it flaps, the more the sound waves it emits pile up.

You can do an experiment proving the Doppler Effect simply by standing on a street corner and listening to the sounds of car and truck tires as they go by. Listen to the difference between the sounds of traffic approaching you and traffic going away from you. Explain why the sounds are different.

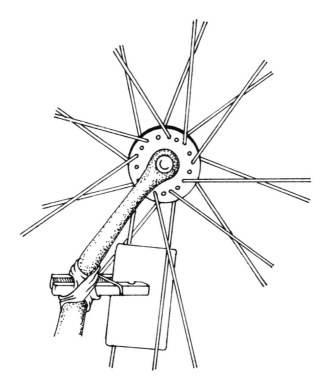

CHAPTER 9

MARIE CURIE
(CHEMISTRY)

O ne of the interesting things about experiments is the time it takes to get results. Many experiments take just a short time. The instant water spilled over the sides of the tub, Archimedes had his answer. When the horses could not pull Von Guericke's hemispheres apart, his experiment was over. He had proved the power of air pressure. It took Galileo just the moment his iron balls fell to the ground to overturn an opinion that had been held for nearly 2000 years. Yet other experiments take a longer time. In fact, one of the great experiments that helped usher in our atomic age took not days, nor even months, but *four* years.

And this isn't all. Although this experiment occurred in the modern era of science, it did not involve a well-equipped laboratory.

Instead, it was done in a leaky shed that had a dirt floor, with equipment consisting of a coal stove, shovels, and iron kettles.

The experiment was conceived and carried out nearly ninety years ago by two of the most famous scientists of history, Pierre and Marie Curie. The Curies were husband and wife. They were beginning their work in a very exciting time for science. The year they were married, 1895, x-rays were discovered by a German physicist, Wilhelm Roentgen. A year later a French physicist, Antoine Becquerel, discovered that uranium constantly gives off rays. Marie Curie was to label this phenomenon "radioactivity".

Before their marriage, Pierre Curie was already one of the most widely known young scientists in France. He made important discoveries concerning heat and magnetism, and with electricity and crystals. The latter discovery led to the development of microphones and gramophones.

Though he was a very good scientist, his wife was a great scientist, one of the greatest scientists ever.

She was born Marie Sklodowska, in Poland, and grew up in poverty and hardship. When she came to the Sorbonne University in Paris, she was so poor that she once fainted in class from hunger.

After she married Pierre, she became interested in the radioactivity of uranium. She used her husband's discoveries with electricity and crystals to measure the radioactivity precisely. She made an important discovery. In some samples, there was much more radioactivity than uranium alone would account for. She concluded that there must be another radioactive substance. Since the substance was too small to be visible, it must be very powerful.

She called the substance radium. In 1898, she and Pierre set about trying to find it. From the beginning, they were faced with enormous problems. If radium was found in such faint traces that it could only be detected by its radioactivity, then a great deal of ore was needed to collect the substance. Not just pounds of ore, but tons of it.

Fortunately, the Curies found such a large quantity. In Europe, pitchblende was mined for uranium salts, used in the manufacturing of glass. Marie had discovered that pitchblende was highly radioactive, even after uranium had been removed.

She was convinced that radium existed in pitchblende. The Curies could not afford to buy pitchblende before the salts were removed. But since the ore was considered worthless after the uranium was removed, it was given to them free, as long as they paid for the cost of hauling it to Paris.

The Curies used all their savings to have pitchblende delivered to a drafty old shed in Paris. There they labored to extract radium. They shoveled the pitchblende into kettles, mixed the material with chemicals, and boiled off the residue.

They labored in the shed for four years. In summer, the heat inside was stifling. In winter, the temperature rarely rose above 50° Fahrenheit. The first winter, Marie caught pneumonia and was ill for three months. Pierre wanted to stop several times, but his wife insisted that they go on.

During this time they also took care of their young child, Irene, who was born a year before they began their work with pitch-blende. Irene would later earn a Nobel Prize herself in chemistry.

Finally, in 1902, after refining about eight tons of pitchblende by hand, the Curies had collected one tenth of a gram of radium.

It was indeed more radioactive than uranium—more than one million times more radioactive.

Marie and Pierre Curie's discovery of the new element radium opened the way to breakthroughs in cancer treatment and to in-creased knowledge of the structure and activities of the atom—knowledge that less than five decades later helped develop the atomic bomb.

For their efforts, the Curies won the Nobel Prize for physics in 1903.

In 1906, Pierre was tragically killed in a carriage accident on a Paris street. Afterward, Marie filled his position of professor at the Sorbonne, becoming the first woman to teach there. She won the Nobel Prize again in 1911 for discovering two new elements.

Marie Curie died in 1934 of leukemia, caused by overexposure to radium, the element that she had unlocked from nature by perform-ing one of the most incredible and courageous experiments ever.

CHAPTER 10

ALEXANDER FLEMING (BIOLOGY)

As we have learned, not all famous experiments are carefully thought out. Some are not even planned at all. They take place accidentally, without the observer knowing an experiment is happening. When Archimedes lowered himself into the bath, he wasn't consciously doing an experiment. When Newton went out to the orchard beside his mother's manor at Woolsthorpe, it wasn't with the idea that a falling apple would prompt him to begin formulating the laws of gravity. These were experiments that flowed from everyday life.

But as the quest for scientific knowledge became more complex, so did experiments to unlock that knowledge. In the sixteenth century, Galileo needed only a high place and two iron balls. In the seventeenth century, Newton only a prism, a window shade, and a screen. In the eighteenth century, Franklin used a ball of kite string, a kite, and a key.

But in the early nineteenth century, Faraday had to build an ingenious apparatus to conduct his experiments in magnetism and electricity. In the latter part of that century, experimental apparatus were too complicated for laymen. In the twentieth century, some experimental equipment—atom smashers, for instance—cost scores of millions of dollars and required hundreds of technicians to operate and maintain them.

But though the apparatus for conducting experiments have become vastly more complicated, the basic principle of the experiment—proving by doing—remains unchanged. Great advances in science still can be achieved by simple, even accidental, actions.

Consider what happened to an obscure biologist one fall day in 1928 in London, England. He was reporting to work as usual at his laboratory, where he was studying bacteria. As he unlocked the door and went into the tiny room filled with test tubes, Bunsen burners, microscopes, and glass dishes, he had no idea that he was on the verge of making one of the most important discoveries of the century. It was a discovery that would have a dramatic impact on our lives.

The biologist was Dr. Alexander Fleming. The forty-seven-year-old Scot had been interested in bacteria for over a decade, since he had been a medical officer in the British Army during the First World War in France. He had treated devastating wounds then. He realized that the harsh antiseptics that were given to help the wounds heal actually benefited the bacteria by killing white cells, which are the body's defense against bacteria. After the war, Fleming directed his efforts to finding bacteria-killing substances. In 1922, he discovered a protein found in tears and mucus that kills bacteria. On that famous day in 1928, he was studying bacteria that caused boils.

Fleming studied bacteria by growing them in cultures on beds of gelatin in tiny glass dishes. The dishes had covers on them so no other organisms could interfere with the cultures' growth. But that morning, he found specks of greenish mold in one of the dishes. That meant that his culture was not pure. Fleming was about to throw the dish away when he looked once more at the specks. Circling each speck was a ring of clear, bacteria-free gelatin.

Fleming examined the mold under a microscope.

Bringing it into focus, he received a shock of surprise. He saw that it was a common mold, the kind often found on stale bread. It belonged to the Penicillium group. That wasn't surprising. What surprised him was that the rings around the mold flecks indicated that the bacteria had been killed.

Fleming set about isolating the mold and introducing it to various kinds of bacteria. He found that it killed some bacteria and not others. He then mixed water with the golden liquid that oozed from the mold and injected the mixture into infected mice. The mice that did not receive the injections died. The mice that got his penicillin injections lived. This meant that penicillin did not kill white cells. Instead, it helped them fight infection.

But Fleming was a biologist, not a chemist. He could not isolate or even describe the exact bacteria-killing substance. Hoping that he might be helped in this effort, he published his findings. But no researchers were interested in his discoveries. Sulfa drugs were just coming into use. They were called wonder drugs. So Fleming's findings were ignored for ten years.

But sulfa drugs did not prove to be as effective as experts once thought they would be. In 1939, with England at war, two British scientists, Howard Florey and Ernst Boris Chain, isolated penicillin. The drug saved thousands of wounded soldiers and became the first antibiotic.

Who knows what the history of medicine might have been if on that day in 1928, Fleming had thrown those mold dishes away!

THE EXPERIMENT:

What you need:

> two saucers
> a piece of bread
> dust from a windowsill

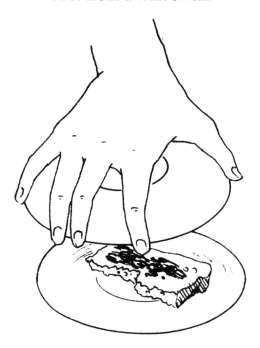

What you do:

You can create the same kind of conditions that Fleming accidentally did when he discovered penicillin. Place the bread—preferably
old, stale bread—on a saucer. Dampen the bread with water. Sprin-
kle dust on the bread. Cover it with the second saucer, place it in a
dark place, and wait three days. Uncover the bread.

During the three days, mold should have grown on the bread. The
mold consists of a grayish fuzz and small black dots. The fuzz are
runners or stems that attach to the bread. The black dots are tiny
sacks.

To get a better view of the mold, you can do what Fleming did.
Look at it under a microscope. With tweezers, put some of the mold

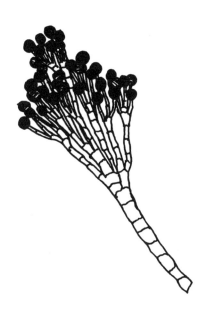

on a drop of water on a slide. Place a cover slip on top of the slide. Now view the mold under different powers.

You will see almost exactly what Fleming saw, the runners and sacks. If you look at the mold under a high enough power, you will see that the runners are tubelike and that tiny spores have spilled from the sacks. These spores are carried on air currents. When they land on something nourishing like bread, they sprout into new molds.

You can conduct a simple experiment to show what kind of environment molds grow best in. This time take three pieces of bread. With the first piece, repeat the previous experiment: dampen the bread and place it between saucers in a dark place. Place the second piece of bread beside the first, but do not cover it. Put the third piece of bread uncovered in a refrigerator. Wait three days. Then examine the bread. Most likely you will find that the first piece of bread has more mold on it than the other two. What does this tell you about what environment molds grow best in?

GLOSSARY

Air pressure the pressure exerted by the weight of air

Antibiotic a chemical produced by fungi or very small organisms that can harm and kill bacteria

Antiseptic something that cleans away or kills germs

Apparatus a complex device that can include instruments, tools, materials, machinery, etc.

Archimedes (287–212 B.C.) a Greek philosopher, mathematician, and inventor

Aristotle (384–322 B.C.) an ancient Greek philosopher

Astronomer a person who scientifically studies the heavens

Bacteria microscopic organisms (See *Organism*)

Antoine Becquerel (1852–1908) a French physicist

Black Death See *Bubonic plague.*

Bubonic plague a form of plague that creates buboes, or swelling of the glands located mainly in the armpits and groin; Black Death is a form of bubonic plague

Calculus a special method of calculating mathematical problems

Ernst Chain (1906–   ) an English biochemist, born in Germany, who won the Nobel Prize for medicine in 1945

Color spectrum a range of colors made when sunlight passes through a prism (See *Prism*); the color spectrum includes red, orange, yellow, green, blue, indigo, and violet

Culture the development of small organisms for study and medical diagnosis

Marie Curie (1867–1935) a Polish physicist and chemist who lived and worked in France

Pierre Curie (1859–1906) a French physicist and chemist

Humphry Davy (1778–1829) an English chemist

Displacement the weight or the volume of a fluid that is removed or displaced by a floating or submerged object

Christian Johann Doppler (1803–1853) an Austrian physicist

Electricity a force that manifests light, heat, attraction, repulsion, and magnetism

Electromagnet iron or steel that is magnetized by electricity passing through coils around it

Equation a mathematical expression proving that two quantities are equal

Experiment a test or action designed to verify an idea, theory, or principle

Michael Faraday (1791–1867) an English physicist and chemist who made important discoveries concerning electricity

Alexander Fleming (1881–1955) a Scottish physician who made important studies of bacteria and molds

Howard Florey (1898–1968) an Australian pathologist who worked in England and won the Nobel Prize for medicine in 1945

Benjamin Franklin (1706–1790) an American inventor, statesman, scientist, and author

Galaxy a large system of stars

Galileo Galilei (1564–1642) an Italian physicist and astronomer

Luigi Galvani (1737–1798) an Italian scientist who first linked chemical reactions to electrical activity

Galvanometer an instrument that detects and records the strength of small electrical currents

Otto Von Guericke a seventeenth-century German burgomaster, inventor, and scientist

Heresy a belief that goes against established church beliefs

Holy Roman Empire an empire located in central Europe and ruled chiefly by German emperors from 962 to 1806

Industrial Revolution the broad and deep changes made in people's lives starting in England around 1760 when machines began to be used in industrial production

Laboratory a place where scientific experiments can be carried out

Leukemia a cancerous disease that causes an overproduction of white blood cells

Leyden jar a jar, lined with tinfoil, that can store an electrical charge

Magnet a piece of iron or steel that attracts certain kinds of metals

Magnetism the force that causes attraction in magnets

Mold furry growth of fungi that can be found on decaying animal or plants

Navigation guiding the direction of land, air, and sea travel

Isaac Newton (1642–1727) an English physicist and mathematician who made important discoveries dealing with gravity, light, motion, and mathematics

63

Nobel Prize a prize awarded each year in each of seven categories: 1) chemistry, 2) physics, 3) medicine, 4) physiology, 5) literature, 6) peace, 7) economics; the prize grows from money and directives in the will of Swedish engineer and manufacturer Alfred Nobel (1833–1896)

Hans Oersted (1777–1851) a Danish physicist

Organism a form of animal or plant life

Pendulum a long, swinging object

Penicillin an antibiotic made from a mold, Penicillium (See *Antibiotic*)

Pitchblende an ore from which uranium and radium can be extracted

Plague a widespread disease that causes many deaths

Prism a clear object that can separate light into the color spectrum (See *Color spectrum*)

Pyramid a large structure of stone with a square or rectangular base and triangular sides that come to a point

Radioactivity the emitting of energy by certain elements in the form of waves and particles

Radium a metallic element that emits radioactivity and that was used in treating cancer and in paints that glow in the dark

Refraction the change of direction of a ray of light, heat, or sound

Wilhelm Roentgen (1845–1923) a German physicist who discovered x-rays

Technician a specially trained person

Uranium a radioactive metallic element

Voltage recorder See *Galvanometer*

BIBLIOGRAPHY

Asimov, Isaac. *Asimov's Biographical Encyclopedia of Science and Technology*. New York: Doubleday and Co., Inc., 1964.

Beeler, Nelson. *Experiments in Sound*. New York: Thomas Y. Crowell Co., 1961.

———. *Experiments with Light*. New York: Thomas Y. Crowell Co., 1957.

Behnke, Frances L. *Magnetism*. New York: Golden Press, Western Publishing Co., 1962.

Beiser, Germaine. *The Story of the Earth's Magnetic Field*. New York: E.P. Dutton, 1964.

Berger, Melvin. *Triumphs of Modern Science*. New York: McGraw-Hill Book Co., 1964.

Complete Guide For Young Experimenters. New York: Sterling Publishing Co., Inc., 1967.

da Andrade, E.N. *Sir Isaac Newton, His Life and Work*. New York: Doubleday and Co., Inc., 1954.

Dunsheath, Percy. *Electricity, How it Works*. New York: Thomas Y. Crowell Co., 1960.

Fisher, S.H. *Table Top Science*. New York: Doubleday and Co., Inc., 1972.

Halacy, Daniel S., Jr. *Radiation, Magnetism, and Living Things*. New York: Holiday House, Inc., 1966.

———. *They Gave Their Names to Science*. New York: G.P. Putnam's Sons, 1967.

Harvey, Tad. *The Quest of Michael Faraday*. New York: Doubleday and Co., Inc., 1961.

Jacobowitz, Henry. *Electricity Made Simple*. New York: Made Simple Books, Inc., 1959.

Keen, Martin. *Let's Experiment*. New York: Grosset and Dunlap, Inc., 1968.

Lee, Dana and Thomas, Henry. *Living Biographies of Great Scientists*. New York: Doubleday and Co., Inc., 1959.

Mandelbaum, Arnold. *Electricity, The Story of Power*. New York: The Putnam Publishing Group, 1960.

Mandell, Muriel. *Physics Experiments for Children*. New York: Sterling Publishing Co., Inc., 1959.

———. *Science for Children*. New York: Sterling Publishing Co., Inc., 1959.

Mann, A.L. and Vivian, A.C. *Famous Physicists*. New York: The John Day Company, 1963.

Math, Irwin. *Wires and Watts*. New York: Charles Scribners and Sons, 1981.

Morgan, Alfred P. *The Pageant of Electricity*. D. Appleton-Century Co., Inc., 1939.

700 Science Experiments for Everyone, Unesco. New York: Doubleday and Co., Inc., 1958.

Sootin, Harry. *Experiments with Electric Currents.* New York: W.W. Norton and Co., Inc., 1969.

————. *Experiments with Static Electricity.* New York: W.W. Norton and Co., Inc., 1969.

————.*Experiments with Water.* New York: Grosset and Dunlap, Inc., 1971.

————. *Michael Faraday.* New York: Julian Messner, 1954.

Turner, Rufus P. *Basic Electricity.* New York: Rinehart and Co., Inc., 1957.

Victor, Edward. *Magnets and Electromagnetics.* Chicago: Benefic Press, 1967.

INDEX

FAMOUS EXPERIMENTS

ABOUT THE AUTHOR

Brent Filson has published twelve young people's books and more than 100 magazine articles, many of which deal with medical and scientific subjects. He currently lives in Massachusetts with his wife and four children.